Alabama

Facts and Symbols

by Emily McAuliffe

Consultant:
Allen T. Cronenberg, Historian
Arts and Humanities Center
Auburn University
Auburn, Alabama

Capstone press
Mankato, Minnesota

Capstone Press
151 Good Counsel Drive, P.O. Box 669, Mankato, Minnesota 56002
http://www.capstone-press.com

Library of Congress Cataloging-in-Publication Data
McAuliffe, Emily.
   Alabama facts and symbols/by Emily McAuliffe.—Rev. and updated ed.
   p. cm.—(The states and their symbols)
   Includes bibliographical references and index.
   Summary: Presents information about the state of Alabama, its nickname, flag, motto, and emblems.
   ISBN 0-7368-2231-3 (hardcover)
   1. Emblems, State—Alabama—Juvenile literature. [1. Emblems, State—Alabama.
2. Alabama.] I. Title. II. Series.
CR203.A65M37 2003
976.1—dc21   2002154050

Editorial Credits
Christianne C. Jones, update editor; Damian Koshnick, editor; Linda Clavel, update
   cover designer and illustrator; Heather Kindseth, cover designer; Kelly Garvin,
   update photo researcher; Kimberly Danger, photo researcher

Photo Credits
James P. Rowan, 22 (middle)
One Mile Up Inc., 8, 10 (inset)
Photo Network/Jim Schwabel, 10; Nancy Hoyt Belcher, 22 (top)
Racking Horse Breeders' Association of America/Sandra Hall, 18
Tom & Pat Leeson, cover
Unicorn Stock Photos/Charles E. Schmidt, 16; Jeff Greenberg, 22 (bottom)
Visuals Unlimited/Inga Spence, 6; Tom J. Ulrich, 12; David Sieren, 14;
   Gerald & Buff Corsi, 20

1 2 3 4 5 6 08 07 06 05 04 03

Table of Contents

Tennessee

Tennessee River

The NASA-Marshall
Space Flight Center

Dismals Canyon

Georgia

● Birmingham

Birmingham Civil
Rights Institute

ALABAMA

Mississippi

Tombigbee River

Alabama River

★ Montgomery

Mobile River

Mobile

Florida

Gulf of Mexico

★ Capital
○ City
🏛 Places to
    Visit
〜 River

Fast Facts

Capital: Montgomery is Alabama's capital.

Largest City: Birmingham is Alabama's largest city. About 242,800 people live in Birmingham.

Size: Alabama covers 52,423 square miles (135,776 square kilometers). Alabama is the 30th largest state.

Location: Alabama is located in the southeastern United States.

Population: About 4,447,100 people live in Alabama (2000 U.S. Census Bureau).

Statehood: Alabama became the 22nd state on December 14, 1819.

Natural Resources: Alabama has coal, marble, and forests.

Manufactured Goods: Workers in Alabama make textiles, steel, and rubber products such as tires.

Crops: Alabama farmers grow peanuts, cotton, and pecans. Livestock farmers raise chickens.

State Name and Nickname

The name Alabama comes from the Choctaw Native American words Alba Amo. These words mean "clearers of the thicket." A thicket is a thick growth of plants, bushes, or small trees. The Choctaw people were once called the Alba Amo.

Alabama's nickname is the Heart of Dixie. Dixie is another name for the southern part of the United States. This nickname means Alabamians are proud to be Southerners.

Some people call Alabama the Cotton State. Farmers throughout Alabama grow cotton. Workers make cloth and other products from this valuable state crop.

Other nicknames come from Alabama's state symbols. Alabama is known as the Camellia State. The camellia (ca-MEEL-ee-a) is Alabama's state flower. Alabama also is known as the Yellowhammer State. The yellowhammer is Alabama's state bird.

Alabama is the 10th largest producer of cotton in the United States. One of its nicknames is the Cotton State.

State Seal and Motto

Alabama officials adopted the state seal in 1939. The seal reminds Alabamians of their state's government. The seal also makes government papers official.

Alabama's state seal shows a map of the state's largest rivers. Rivers were important to Alabama's farmers and lumberjacks. Farmers sent their cotton to market by boat. Lumberjacks floated logs down Alabama's rivers to mills. Mill workers cut these logs into lumber for building.

In 1817, Alabama's government adopted a territorial seal. The present state seal is the same as Alabama's old territorial seal.

In 1939, Alabama officials adopted the state motto "We Dare Maintain Our Rights." This motto means Alabamians will fight for the freedom to make their own decisions.

Some of Alabama's largest rivers appear on the state seal.

Alabama's capitol building is in Montgomery. This city became Alabama's capital in 1846. Government officials meet in the capitol to make the state's laws.

Workers built Alabama's first state capitol in 1847. A fire destroyed the building in 1849. Builders finished the current capitol in 1851. They built it on the same site as the first capitol. Alabama sylacauga marble covers the outside of the capitol. Sylacauga is a type of rock found in Alabama.

Alabama officials adopted the state flag in 1895. The flag is white with a dark red *X* across it. This *X* is known as the cross of St. Andrew.

By 1861, 11 states had left the United States to form their own nation. These states called themselves the Confederate States of America. Montgomery was the capital of the Confederacy.

Alabama's state flag was made to look like the flag used for the 11 Confederate States of America.

State Bird

In 1927, Alabama adopted the yellowhammer as its state bird. People also call yellowhammers flickers or yellow-shafted woodpeckers. These birds are common in Alabama. Yellowhammers are named for their color. Their bodies are yellow and gray. A red patch covers their necks.

Yellowhammers often build nests in dead trees. Female yellowhammers lay one egg each day for 6 to 10 days. The eggs hatch in about 17 days. Yellowhammers grow to be about 11 inches (28 centimeters) long.

Alabama soldiers who fought in the Civil War were called yellowhammers. The soldiers' uniforms were yellow and gray like the birds' feathers. The soldiers even stuck yellowhammer feathers in their shirts and hats. Alabama and the other Confederate states fought for independence during the Civil War (1861-1865).

Yellowhammers eat mostly ants and other insects.

13

State Tree

In 1949, Alabama officials chose the longleaf pine as the state tree. This tree grows mostly in the central and southern parts of the state.

Longleaf pine leaves are branches of needles. The longleaf pine gets its name from the way its leaves grow when the tree is young. The leaves of a young longleaf pine grow longer than the leaves of most pine trees. A young longleaf pine's leaves grow up to 2 feet (61 centimeters) long.

As a longleaf pine grows, its leaves shorten to about half of their original length. The pine loses its long-leaf look as its branches grow.

Longleaf pines are conifers. Conifers have cones that hold the trees' seeds. Longleaf pines have large, prickly cones that grow 5 to 10 inches (13 to 25 centimeters) long.

Longleaf pines can grow to be 130 feet (40 meters) tall. They can live to be 300 years old.

State Flower

In 1959, government officials made the camellia Alabama's state flower. Many different types and colors of camellias grow in Alabama. Officials did not choose any specific camellia as the official state flower.

Camellia flowers can have white, pink, or red petals. Some camellia flowers have red and white stripes. Many Alabamians prefer red and white camellias. These are the colors of the Alabama state flag.

Camellia blossoms can grow as large as 5 inches (13 centimeters) across. In Alabama, these plants bloom nine months of the year. Many Alabamians use camellia plants to decorate their yards and gardens.

Camellia flowers grow on evergreen bushes. These plants keep their green leaves year round. The camellia bush can grow to be 40 feet (12 meters) tall.

Alabamians make teas from some types of camellia plants.

State Animal

Alabamians chose the racking horse as the state animal in 1975. The racking horse is named for its smooth walk. Alabamians call this stride a rack. The stride of the racking horse also is called a single-foot gait because only one foot strikes the ground at a time.

Racking horses are smaller than most horses. An adult racking horse measures about 5 feet (1.5 meters) tall at the shoulders. A racking horse usually weighs about 1,000 pounds (454 kilograms). Racking horses have long, sloping necks and strong backs.

In the 1800s, many plantation owners rode racking horses. These farmers used racking horses to supervise work on their large farms. Racking horses are calm and comfortable to ride for long periods of time. They also are strong and can run at a fast pace for long distances.

Racking horses can be black, brown, red-brown, and sometimes spotted.

State Insect: Alabama's state insect is the monarch butterfly. The state adopted this symbol in 1989. Monarch butterflies have orange and black wings with white spots.

State Mascot and Butterfly: The eastern tiger swallowtail became Alabama's state mascot and butterfly in 1989. In Alabama, this large, yellow butterfly stands for good luck.

State Reptile: In 1990, Alabama's government adopted the red-bellied turtle as the state reptile. This turtle does not live anywhere else in the world.

State Rock: In 1969, Alabama officials named marble the state rock. Alabama marble is known for its strength and bright white color.

State Saltwater Fish: In 1955, Alabamians chose the fighting tarpon as the state saltwater fish. Tarpons live near Alabama's shore in the Gulf of Mexico. People in Alabama fish for the large, silver tarpon.

Adult red-bellied turtles are about 12 inches (30 centimeters) in length. They often sun themselves on logs near water.

Places to Visit

Birmingham Civil Rights Institute

The Birmingham Civil Rights Institute is located in Birmingham. This center educates people about the history of civil and human rights in the United States. Visitors learn about civil rights through films, exhibits, and galleries.

Dismals Canyon

Dismals Canyon is near Phil Campbell. This area has one of the oldest forests east of the Mississippi River. Visitors walk along this dark, misty canyon and see waterfalls and cliffs. Artifacts found on the canyon floor show that humans lived there 10,000 years ago.

The NASA-Marshall Space Flight Center

The NASA-Marshall Space Flight Center is in Huntsville. Workers at the center build equipment and do tests for the space program. Visitors see rockets from the past. They also tour buildings where workers make parts for space stations.

Words to Know

canyon (KAN-yuhn)—a valley with steep sides
Confederacy (kuhn-FED-ur-uh-see)—the 11 Southern states that left the United States in 1860 and 1861 to form a new nation
conifer (KON-uh-fur)—an evergreen tree that produces cones; the longleaf pine is a conifer.
gait (GATE)—a way of walking
lumberjack (LUHM-bur-jak)—a person who cuts down trees in order to make lumber; lumber is used for building.
stride (STRIDE)—a long step

Read More

Brown, Dottie. *Alabama.* Hello U.S.A. Minneapolis: Lerner Publications, 2002.

Kummer, Patricia K. *Alabama.* One Nation. Mankato, Minn.: Capstone Press, 2003.

Parker, Janice. *Alabama.* A Kid's Guide to American States. Mankato, Minn.: Weigl Publishers, 2001.

Shirley, David. *Alabama.* Celebrate the States. New York: Benchmark Books, 2000.

Useful Addresses

Alabama Archives and History
624 Washington Avenue
Montgomery, AL 36130-0100

Alabama Bureau of Tourism and Travel
401 Adams Avenue Suite 126
Montgomery, AL 36104

Internet Sites

Do you want to find out more about Alabama?
Let FactHound, our fact-finding hound dog, do the
research for you.

Here's how:
1) Visit **http://www.facthound.com**
2) Type in the **BOOK ID** number:
   0736822313
3) Click on **FETCH IT**.

FactHound will fetch Internet sites picked by
our editors just for you!

Index